FROM
NOW ON

FROM NOW ON

A LENT COURSE ON
HOPE AND REDEMPTION IN
THE *GREATEST SHOWMAN*

RACHEL MANN

DARTON · LONGMAN + TODD

With profound gratitude to those members
of St Nicholas, Burnage whose comments and
participation in home groups made this course
immeasurably better than it otherwise
would have been.

First published in 2018 by
Darton, Longman and Todd Ltd
1 Spencer Court
140–142 Wandsworth High Street
London SW18 4JJ

Reprinted 2019

ISBN 978-0-232-53392-7

A catalogue record for this book is available from the British Library.

Camera logo by Senhikari Studio/shutterstock.com
Designed and produced by Judy Linard
Printed and bound in Great Britain by Bell & Bain, Glasgow

CONTENTS

INTRODUCTION

The Bible suggests that, in the beginning, God created the world and saw it was good (Genesis 1:1-3). Given how often religious people tell us that the world is a fallen place, full of sin and in need of redemption, to remember that God finds his created world delightful is an important corrective. The modern poet Glyn Maxwell suggests that, as our ancestors left the trees and began to spread across the African plains and savannahs, they 'looked upon' the world and saw it was good.[1] In short, our ancestors apprehended the beauty of the world and were filled with delight. In a world which is full of challenges, pain and insecurity, it can be very difficult to keep hold of this vision. It's very easy to fall into cynicism and selfishness and meanness. If the Bible is appropriately realistic about the tragic limits of human beings, it is always worth remembering that – from God's point of view – there is so much about the world that should fill us with hope, faith and love. The world remains the stuff on which dreams are made.

The Greatest Showman has become something of a popular culture phenomenon. It has generated singalongs, parties and countless repeat viewings. After a slow start at the box office on the back of critical panning, it became the most successful film in UK cinema of 2018. Its tale of Phineas T. Barnum and his Circus has chimed with a world hungry for both hope and for fun, not least because it shows a world in which

---

[1] Glyn Maxwell, *On Poetry* (Harvard: Harvard University Press, 2013).

being an outsider is no bar to success and respect. Above all, it is a film that brings delight to the forefront and is unafraid of dreaming. In a scary world, shaped by aggressive regimes and authoritarian leaders, it is perhaps unsurprising that *The Greatest Showman* has generated such a devoted following. Indeed, though it is a highly-fictionalised account of Barnum's life, it manages to offer a powerful echo of God's original delight in the world and his ongoing desire for us to celebrate his creation.

This film may seem a curious subject for a Lent book. The great themes of Lent – the longing for justice and mercy, the invitation to sober reflection on sin, and, most of all, the call for repentance – might strike us as very far away from those found in *The Greatest Showman*. Where the weeks of Lent traditionally represent a time of preparation for the joy of Easter, it might be suggested that *The Greatest Showman* wants to skip that reflection and leap too readily to the joy. If there are grounds for that claim, I want to counter with two thoughts: firstly, if *The Greatest Showman* mostly takes place in a 'major key', its power lies in contrast. When Barnum loses sight of what has made him a success and begins to stray from the path of faithfulness (to his family and beliefs), the film very much enters a 'minor key' shaped around doubt and betrayal. Furthermore, if the mood of the film is 'joy', it is one tempered by the ups-and-downs of Barnum, his friends' and his family's lives. In short, the film is not so much about mindless pleasure or happiness, but deep joy. This is closer to the joy we find in the Christian faith – the joy shaped through the Cross and God's truth – than a fleeting happiness often offered by the world.

If, as I believe, this is a book which lends itself to study all year around, behind the bright and shiny chords of this musical's songs are universal themes which chime with Lent. Most of all, *The Greatest Showman* asks, what does hope and love look like in a world which so readily tramples on those dreams? It frames that question through the lens of those considered outsiders, either because of poverty, class, disability, ethnicity and visual stereotyping. Jesus' story speaks powerfully into this, not least because arguably his ministry represents a dramatic statement that those society considers 'outsiders', that is, those who are treated as 'other' and 'second-rate', are 'centre-stage' in God's love. Jesus lives as one on the edges of respectable society and dies a criminal's death. As God's Son among us, it is as powerful a sign of God's priorities as we can imagine.

This book, then, is an invitation to enjoy a delightful film, but also to look closer. Behind the shiny and sometimes overwhelming show tunes, is a story with real heart and imagination. If it is tempting to read Barnum as a Jesus-like saviour figure – what is sometimes called (with a serious critical intent) a 'White Saviour Figure', who uses his privilege to help the 'less-fortunate' – the story is more nuanced. It is much more about the power of outsider communities to claim hope and faith and love. Barnum is a deeply flawed character who is more like Peter or one of the other disciples than Jesus. As the film unfolds, we discover that it is the members of the Circus who hold the power to transform the world, rather than Barnum. *The Greatest Showman* opens vistas for people of faith and none to reflect on the nature of faith, hope and love. By taking time over the coming weeks to watch and re-watch this film slowly, I hope you will see how the story of Barnum and his Circus reveals Christian themes of hope and dreams, family and community, respectability and resistance, betrayal and redemption. Just as the outsider community around Barnum 'comes alive', I pray that this study guide helps your faith and thinking come alive.

HOW TO USE THIS BOOK

There are few hard and fast rules when it comes to working with the material in this book. However, it does assume that both individuals and groups will have watched *The Greatest Showman* before the course commences. It may be worth inviting participants – whether they're familiar with the film or not – to meet for an opening 'pre-course' session in which all can watch the film together. Every course member should have a copy of the book so that they can reflect on the material between meetings and go over material that has not been covered due to time constraints. If everyone is already familiar with the film, it may be worth treating this initial meeting as a singalong party. It will give participants an opportunity to socialise, get to know each other, and begin to chat about the key themes in the film. Some, of course, may find the idea of a 'singalong party' a little inappropriate while exploring Lent; if so, then don't do it. However, do not be surprised if the excess of joy in the film leads to people singing and dancing along.

Beyond that expectation, the aim of this book is to provide an abundance of resources that may be used across the forty days of Lent. As with many other Lent books, it is divided into five sections or weeks, on the assumption that it shall be used for house groups and Lent groups meeting once a week in preparation for Holy Week and Easter. For groups following this pattern, it's worth saying – if this book is used carefully and thoughtfully – there will almost certainly be too much material to be properly covered in a standard one-and-a-half or two-hour session. This is deliberate. Firstly, this course works best when the leader/s reflect beforehand on what elements should be included in each session and make decisions about what might be included or left out. Secondly, it is hoped that, between sessions, participants will dig deeper into the wider material offered in this book.

If this book has been written with groups in mind, it will also reward individual study and, in many ways, will come alive in a different way when individuals follow its pattern. The advantage of individual study is flexibility: private study readily lends itself to reflection broken up across times and days. While concentrated study remains the most focussed way of prayerful reflection, in a busy world, 'dipping in and out' of this book may be the only realistic way of engaging with it. Equally, if this book has been produced for Lenten study, the themes of *The Greatest Showman* have a power and quality which speak far beyond Lent. This book could just as easily be used for monthly study by Home Groups.

Whatever pattern is followed, it is worth restating something that should be obvious: the richest form of devotional study is one that is structured through prayer. Prayer, in its many forms, represents the basic building-block of the Christian disciple's life. The aim of this course is to be fun and thoughtful, but it is constructed as a prayerful activity. I hope you won't treat the opening and closing prayers included in this book as optional extras, unless – of course – the course leaders have other prayers in mind. Should you use this book as an individual, I hope you will be able to structure it into your wider prayer life and tradition, whether that be silence, keeping an Office or structured through your Daily Quiet Time.

One other brief note. It should be acknowledged that using film in study can exclude those with visual impairments. Every effort should be made to include and facilitate the participation of those whose sight is impaired. One of our parish home groups has a member who is significantly visually impaired. We seek to always provide subtitles during viewings and the very best sound system possible. Some DVDs and Blu-Ray offer audio description facilities.

AN HISTORICAL NOTE: BARNUM …
BETWEEN FACT AND FICTION

The simple fact of the matter is that *The Greatest Showman* is – at best – loosely based on the life story of Phineas T. Barnum. For some, especially those who like 'biopic' films to stick to historical fact as closely as possible, this will diminish the value of the film. That attitude, if understandable, might matter if *The Greatest Showman* was trying to be a full-on biopic or documentary, but its purpose is quite different. First and foremost, it's entertainment and there's no harm in that. It's a powerful and kinetic example of story-telling that gathers its power from the way it tells a story of human hope. If it's unhelpful to hold *The Greatest Showman* to the standards of history or biography, a little historical background may help some to see where the film both connects with and departs from Barnum's biography.

Phineas Taylor Barnum was born on 5 July 1810 in Bethel, Connecticut, the son of an innkeeper and tailor. The tailor connection is mirrored in the film, where the young Barnum is shown visiting the home of his future love, Charity, with his tailor father. In the film, he is presented as desperately poor and, following his father's death, is made destitute and homeless. It's a powerful plot device, but it's pure bunkum. Barnum's father died when Phineas was just 15, but young Phineas didn't end up on the streets. He supported his mother and five siblings by doing odd jobs, including managing a boarding house. He led a relatively settled, middle-class life and became a shop keeper. He did marry Charity, but it did not emerge out of some illicit childhood romance. They married when he was 21 and she 19 and they went on to have four daughters.

Romance and family life is at the heart of *The Greatest Showman*. These themes and plot devices create momentum and tension in the film, but they are not faithful to the historical Barnum's story. Charity and Barnum were married for forty-four years, and he said that the day he married her he became 'the husband of the best woman in the world.' However, Barnum's life was taken up with business ventures and Charity's life centred on child-rearing. Equally, while it is true that Barnum promoted the 'Swedish Nightingale' Jenny Lind's tour of the United States, there is no evidence of a relationship or infatuation between them. Lind attempted to leave show-business at 28, but Barnum convinced her to embark on a one-hundred-and-fifty night tour. While there is no evidence of romance between the two, Barnum's promotion of her in the USA, where she was practically unknown, verged on genius. The scene in which she receives universal acclaim is grounded in fact.

Barnum's move into the Museum and Show business was not as presented in the movie. The trigger to get into show-business was the decision of Connecticut's state legislature to ban the state lottery. His shop business had depended on the income and without it his work was unviable. He sold up, moved his family to New York in 1836 and started a variety troupe, *Barnum's Grand Scientific and Musical Theater*, to mixed success. A national financial crisis in 1837 placed his business under immense pressure for several years, a situation only turned around when he took over *Scudder's American Museum* and reinvented it as *Barnum's American Museum*.

Much is made in the film about Barnum's bold recruitment strategies for his show. Barnum's show is presented not so much as exploitative as a way for those who are mocked and abused by society to claim their power and dignity. The extent to which the historical Barnum offered this is moot. Consider, Charles Stratton aka General Tom Thumb. In the film, Stratton is 22 years old; in fact, Barnum recruited him at the age of 4! They were distant cousins, and if we may be shocked by the way Barnum worked a young child in his show, there is some evidence that Stratton changed the perception of circuses. Audiences began to see that those who didn't fit society's norms were not simply to be objectified as 'freaks'. Yet, if the film portrays Barnum as a champion of respect and acceptance for those who are different to societal norms, history suggests otherwise. Most shocking of all is the story of how he got his break in show-business: he exploited an elderly slave-woman, Joice Heth, who he passed off as George Washington's one-hundred-and-sixty-one year-old nurse. When she died, it was revealed she was (only) eighty or so years old. He was a businessman who enjoyed making money and sometimes needed quick money to pay off debts.

Barnum's museum did burn down, on several occasions. On the first occasion in 1865, it was said that two whales were boiled alive. However, there is no evidence that the building was burned down by rioters, although the 'confederate army of New York' attempted to burn it down in 1864. If finding out more about the historical Barnum might make us uncomfortable and affect how we read *The Greatest Showman*, it should not destroy its power. The film is not intended as a historical documentary or a faithful biography. Ultimately it takes Barnum's story as a leaping off point for a very modern reading of the 'business that is show'; this is a world in which creativity and difference combine to set free the human spirit.

Part of this film is about claiming power for ourselves. It challenges a world that seeks to define who we are on the basis of how we look, or where we come from. At one point, the bearded lady Lettie Lutz, sings, 'I'm not scared to be seen, I make no apologies, this is me.' It is a powerful response to a world that would judge her – and all of us – on unfair grounds. If the real-life Barnum failed to live the kind of life we might hope, the world of *The Greatest Showman* argues that we are not to be judged by how the world stereotypes, but celebrated for inner convictions which lead us to the truth. Arguably, it commits Barnum, Lettie and the others to a Way that resists the limits of this world and aims to live through God's vision for us. This vision invites us to live as people who show forth the image of God and who can grow into the likeness of Christ. The story of the historical Barnum can enrich and question this claim, but – on the film's own terms – cannot diminish it.

WEEK 1

'A Million Dreams'

TO START YOU THINKING

'In the last days, God says,
I will pour out my Spirit on all people.
Your sons and daughters will prophesy,
your young men will see visions,
your old men will dream dreams.' (Acts 2:17)

Dreams have fascinated us for thousands of years. The Greeks and the Romans believed that dreams were a way for the gods or dead ancestors to speak to the living. There is evidence that the earliest known civilisations wrote down and sought to interpret dreams, thousands of years before Jesus Christ. And, of course, the Bible includes many famous examples of dreams acting as messages from God to chosen individuals or his chosen people.

As we hear in the Scripture quoted above, on the Day of Pentecost, St Peter stands up and addresses the crowd using words from the Prophet Joel. It's a famous quote that we shall return to in this week's session, but perhaps the most famous biblical dreams, in popular culture, are those given to Joseph – he of the technicolour dreamcoat fame – which enable him to steer the fate of both Egypt and of his family. There are others, not least, that of Joseph's father Jacob. In it, Jacob dreams of the 'ladder' between earth and heaven. Dreams are not limited to the Hebrew Bible. In Matthew's Gospel, we have a cluster of dreams around Jesus' birth (including, the warning to St Joseph about fleeing Herod's wrath). The Joseph of the New Testament acts as an analogue to the Joseph of the Old Testament: through dreams God steers the destiny of the people of God.

Sleeping dreams are a universal part of human experience. The average adult has three to five dreams per night, and each one lasts between a few seconds and twenty to thirty minutes. Most take place during rapid eye movement (REM) sleep and researchers suggest that dreaming is an essential part of healthy living. What dreams might mean is another matter entirely! Dream interpretation is as old as civilisation and the Bible reveals how seriously our forebears took dreams. In the stories of the people of God, dreams become a means for God to speak to mortals and guide his people's destiny. Some dreams are warnings (as when St Joseph is warned about Herod's intention to kill the Messiah), others are visions of a deeper reality (as when Jacob dreams of the Ladder between Heaven and Earth), and some offer practical wisdom. In the First Book of Kings, God appears to Solomon in a dream and offers him anything he desires. Solomon asks for Wisdom, rather than wealth or long-life. It enables Solomon to rule over the people of God with considerable skill, but theologically also indicates his closeness to God: in the Old Testament, Wisdom is often identified with the Spirit of God herself.

In our day and age, dreams have often been interpreted as revealing our deepest desires and needs. Since the work of psychotherapists Sigmund Freud and Carl Jung, 'dream interpretation' has often been placed in a therapeutic context; in Freud's case, a whole theory about dreams being a highway to the Unconscious was developed, and – as almost everyone will know – much of his work centred on interpreting dreams as revealing our sexual drives or, in his later work, what he called the 'death drive'. Thankfully, we don't need to be experts in dream interpretation or Freudian theory to reflect with confidence on the universal human fact of dreaming and our desire to make sense of them. If dreaming is something we often do in idle moments or when we sleep, it also represents one of the grand themes of human life. The musician Ray Charles said, 'dreams, if they are any good, are always a little bit crazy.' Arguably, his point holds good when we think of the way our world has been shaped by people who've dared to dream and act on that dream. Being realistic certainly helps us get through the day, but dreaming – whether they be nocturnal sleeping dreams or visions of possibility – can help us change the world.

Thus, there is a story that Einstein's famous $E=MC^2$ formula came to him in a dream. Mary Shelley's idea for *Frankenstein* and his monster also came to her in a dream, and Paul McCartney dreamed the melody for his famous song, *Yesterday*. Leaving aside sleeping dreams, where might our world be without those who've taken a vision or an idea and attempted to live on them? Some might say it would be in a better place, for not all visions are good or equal! However, the vision or dream of everything from Universal Suffrage to equality between LGBT and straight people starts somewhere and requires corporate action. Shakespeare wrote, 'We are such things as dreams are made on', but without public and community action, dreams and visions fade. More recently, Martin Luther King's famous 'I have a dream' speech has acted as a rallying cry to those seeking civil rights in an unjust world.

In this week's session, we explore how Barnum and Charity live as people with 'a million dreams' and how Barnum's vision enables him to begin to create new possibilities for himself and others. The film reveals how difficult it can be to hold on to our dreams in the face of life's hard knocks. It offers us an opportunity to reflect on how faithful we've been to the dreams we've cherished in our lives and, most especially, how we can live on God's vision for us.

Perhaps Jesus Christ is the greatest dreamer of them all. He teaches us of a vision of the Kingdom of God or Heaven and how we are called to commit to its coming amongst us. In two thousand years, there have been so many false starts and wrong turns, but for Christians 'the Kingdom' remains a living vision. The prophet Joel wrote, 'Then afterward I will pour out my spirit on all flesh; your sons and your daughters shall prophesy, your old men shall dream dreams, and your young men shall see visions.' It remains a challenge and an inspiration to us as people of faith to dare to live on God's promises: to dream and have visions, and dare to act on them.

PRAYER

Wondrous God, we thank you for your abundant love
    which invites us to find the fullness of life in you.
If we are dust and to dust we shall return,
    help us to know we are fearfully and wonderfully
    made,
    crowned with glory and honour.
Help us to receive faith, hope and love as gift
    and when we mar your divine image,
    may we hear your voice as you call us back home.
Enable us, through your Spirit, to be people of dreams
    and visions,
    alert to the call of your Kingdom of Grace and
Peace. Amen

Read
Joel 2:28

Icebreaker
Many people have unusual or ambitious dreams when

they are children or teenagers. Some people want to be an actor, or train driver or astronaut. I wanted to be a nun because I loved *The Sound of Music*. Later on, I wanted to be an archaeologist because I'd seen Indiana Jones in *Raiders of the Lost Ark*! If you feel able, share one of your childhood or youthful dreams. Did you manage to make good on your dream? Did life get in the way?

WATCH

From Opening Credits to the end of 'A Million Dreams', where Charity is revealed to be pregnant (This is a substantial set of scenes, so sit back, relax and enjoy! From: 0.00 to 10.51 mins)

At the beginning of the film, we see Barnum at the height of his powers. Then, the scene dissolves to take us into his back story which reveals the poverty and precariousness of his upbringing as the son of a tailor. Barnum's father works for powerful men, and we discover how Barnum meets the girl of his dreams. While his father makes a suit for Mr Hallett, a powerful man, Barnum meets Hallett's frustrated daughter, Charity, and they both dream of a different life together. During the song 'A Million Dreams' they explore their hopes and dreams for life, including living together in a grand house. As reality intrudes, Barnum's father dies, leaving him penniless, and he becomes homeless. Charity is sent away to Finishing School. Yet, they continue to dream and, through thick and thin, they keep in touch. When Barnum returns, they marry and live a precarious life together, trusting that their love and dreams will see them through. As this scene closes, Charity is expecting the couple's first child.

Think about
To what extent is dreaming and having visions of a better future part of human identity? Are children particularly gifted at vision?

The person who helps the youthful Barnum when he is at his lowest is an outsider. Do those on the margins or edges have any specific insights into the importance of solidarity and hope?

How difficult is it to maintain a childhood vision? Are young people inclined to be dismissed and disbelieved? What changes as we get older?

GOING DEEPER

Read
1 Samuel 3:1-9
'The Calling of Samuel'

In this reading we perceive a gap between the Human and the Divine. The young Samuel – who will later grow up to be a great prophet and leader – hears God calling in the night and yet his mentor Eli does not recognise it. The scene becomes almost comedic as Samuel is repeatedly sent back to sleep by his mentor. It is only after God has called three times – a motif that is repeated in the Bible – that Eli understands.

Samuel offers an example of obedience to God's call – 'Here I am'. There is a simplicity in Samuel's response, that perhaps is easier when we are children.

Later in the First Book of Samuel, we discover as God speaks to Samuel, that God plans to bring down the corrupt house of Eli and all he has built. It takes enormous courage on Samuel's part to speak the truth to the powerful grown-up Eli.

Both Barnum and Samuel are persistent in their faithfulness to their 'dreams'. It can be very hard to be as persistent in modern life. What are the things that get in the way of us making a response to God's invitation and call on our lives?

The rock band Green Day sang about a 'Boulevard of Broken Dreams'. Have any of us ever had the experience of having a sense of vocation or call crushed or turned down? If so, what was your response?

Who are the people who've encouraged you in your faith journey? How have you encouraged others? What can we learn from Samuel's example?

WATCH

How life presents threats to our dreams and can (almost) destroy them … (From: 10.53 to 15.37 mins)

In this scene, Barnum is living a life of monotonous drudgery as a shipping clerk at J.W. Mercantile. He sees a deadly future unfold before him, from office to grave. In response, he decides to share his vision with his boss and is rebuffed. He and his co-workers are told that the ships the company owns have all been destroyed. A cruel world intervenes into Barnum's dreams. However, in a moment of enterprising opportunism, Barnum steals the deeds to these destroyed ships. We see that Barnum and Charity now have two daughters, and when he arrives home he initially conceals the bad news and protects his daughters by performing a magic trick that allows them dreams. He has nothing left except his storytelling gifts. Barnum is inspired by his daughters to keep dreaming.

Think about

What do we need for us to have hope? When given the chance to make a wish, Charity says, 'I wish for Happiness forever, just like this.' Is Charity's wish ridiculous? What do we need for happiness?

Is Charity more sensible than Barnum? She finds happiness and contentment in relationship, whereas Barnum seems to be forever striving. Is one approach better than the other?

How close is hope to delusion? How close is magic to foolishness? Have you ever faced a situation when you've struggled to keep a dream alive? What helped?

GOING DEEPER

Read
Matthew 6:25-34
'Do not worry...'

This is justly one of the most famous passages in the Gospels. Jesus seems to suggest that as people called to trust God, we should not be worried about possessions or clothes or food. In short, God will provide for his people.

What does this passage teach us about the Way of Christ and our calling in the world?

Barnum and Charity seem to have very specific wishes and dreams. As people of faith, what are we called to wish for, and how might we fulfil God's dreams?

Who gets their dreams fulfilled in this cruel world? Is the world unjust?

What is God's vision for this world and how can we get involved? Offer some examples of ways God's vision might be made more concrete in the world. What part can we play?

WATCH

Barnum recovers his dream and begins to assemble a cast of outsiders to create a show unlike any seen before (From: 17.54 to 24.20 mins – just before the song 'Come Alive').

Prior to this scene, Barnum has visited the bank to get a loan to purchase the *Museum of American Curiosities*. He meets a future member of his circus, Charles, a grown man who is sufficiently small to be mistaken for a child. Barnum gets the loan by lying about his assets – he has the deeds to the ships, which are of course worthless – and buys a museum he calls *Barnum's American Museum of American Curiosities*. However, despite Barnum's enthusiasm, it is a false start and there is no interest in what he offers.

It's Barnum's daughters who see past the surface to the truth: one of them says, 'You have too many dead things in your museum ... you need something sensational ...' Barnum remembers an act of kindness from his childhood when an outsider gave him an apple when he was at his lowest point. He remembers meeting Charles, the man of limited stature, and seeks to recruit him and others to his project. Barnum tells Charles that when the people see him they'll see a soldier and rather than laugh, they'll salute.

Think about

Is Barnum an exploiter or a visionary? Or a little of

both? What evidence do you have for your position?

As he recruits for his circus, Barnum gives his workers new names and exaggerates their abilities. Is he being a con-man, or does he give excluded people something to live up to?

Are there modern equivalents? *The X-Factor*? *Love Island*? *Britain's Got Talent*? Or would these comparisons do a disservice to Barnum's motivations?

Have any of us ever struggled with our 'self-image'? What is that experience like? If you are able, share a little of that experience with the group. What are the things that enable us to live well and accept ourselves and others as 'talented ... extraordinary ... unique ... beautiful ...'?

GOING DEEPER

Read
Luke 5:27-32
'The calling of Levi ...'

In this reading, Jesus calls Levi, a tax collector, to be one of his disciples. Levi follows him and provides a lavish banquet for Jesus at which tax collectors are present. Others call Jesus out and ask why he is eating with tax collectors and sinners. Jesus responds that he has not called the righteous but the sinful to repentance.

Earlier in Luke 5 (1-11) Jesus has called his first disciples – Peter, Andrew, James and John. Like Barnum, in time, he will give some new names and invite them into new identities: 'You shall become fishers of men'. What differences are there between Barnum's and Jesus' 'call'?

How is God calling you into new and richer relationships? Can you give examples?

In the section we've just read, Jesus calls a tax-collector to become one of his followers. Levi – who is traditionally identified with St Matthew – belongs to a despised trade, not least because it operated on the interface between Jews and the Romans. Tax collectors were considered ritually problematic by some. What does this scene tell us about Jesus?

How do you respond to Jesus' claim that he has not come for the righteous, but to call sinners to repentance? Has Jesus lost the plot?

(Would it be helpful if we thought of 'sinners' less as the religiously immoral or 'outcast' from the synagogue/Temple, but as Jewish biblical scholar Amy-Jill Levine suggests, as referring to wealthy people who do not attend to the poor. Levine says, 'In a first century context, sinners, like tax-collectors are individuals who have removed themselves from the common welfare, who look to themselves rather than the community' (Amy-Jill Levine, *Short Stories by Jesus*, HarperCollins 2015, p.33).

What does the reading tell us about our call or vocation as Christians?

LOOKING AHEAD...
ACTIVITIES TO
CONSIDER THIS
WEEK

Hopefully, this week's session has invited you to reflect not only on your personal dreams and hopes, but how you might pay greater attention to God's call on your life and the communities of which you are part.

It is often only when we look back on our life that we perceive the moments when God has been close to us or challenged us to be more fired up for justice and so on.

A useful activity is to create a timeline of your life on which you mark the big moments of your journey – good and bad – and explore where God has encouraged, challenged or deepened your faith and witness.

By engaging in this activity, you may discover surprising and exciting ways to reengage with God's vision and take up the threads of hope, dreams and justice in your own pilgrimage.

CLOSING PRAYER

Abundant God, Creator of All,
  in the depth of your love
  you empty yourself into our world
  and invite us into the fullness of life.

Whether we have much faith or little,
    help us to hear your call
    and respond with boldness and trust,
    that we may dare to follow you
    wherever you call us. Amen

WEEK 2

'Come Alive'

TO START YOU THINKING

For people living in the wealthy countries of the Economic North, the phrase 'nuclear family' will be very familiar. It emerged after the Second World War to describe one basic picture of what a family is: a father, a mother and their children, all living together in one dwelling place. The word 'nuclear' was not used because of any reference to atomic weapons, but because all members of this kind of family are derived from the same basic 'core' or 'nux'. For many people the idea of a nuclear family remains their dominant image of family: a married heterosexual couple who raise children together. It's an image that has exercised magic over social policy, including various governments promoting it as an ideal of stability and providing the 'best' environment in which to raise children. Financial breaks have often been given to heterosexual married couples who have children. Mainstream churches have also bought into this picture of family, promoting heterosexual marriage and the nuclear family as both ideal and sacred.

One of the fascinating and striking themes of *The Greatest Showman* is its reconfiguration of family and relationship. Certainly, it offers a classic example of a nuclear family at its heart, that of Barnum and Charity and their children, but that itself is read through richer ideas. For, as the film unfolds, the Circus becomes an extended family for outsiders and outcasts. When the circus comes under threat from rowdy elements later in the film, the whole circus acts as one family to defend two of its members, Carlyle and W.D. The Circus becomes a place where those who have struggled in 'ordinary' society – even high society playboy Carlyle – find a place where they can thrive.

In some ways, *The Greatest Showman's* reconfiguration of the idea of family, acts as a reminder that the modern obsession with the nuclear family is just that: an obsession. It represents one version of family, among others. Indeed, it is not one that would have always been recognised by our Christian forebears, especially those of Jesus time. Indeed, for a first century Jew like Jesus, some modern ideas about family would have seemed very curious, indeed (and not necessarily the ones we might think!). Thus, it may surprise some of us to read that the dominant picture of family in Jesus's world was different to ours. In a world dominated by Greek and Roman ideas, the 'familias' was fundamentally based on the rule of a *Paterfamilias* – a dominant male who was the owner and keeper of the estate. Family in this world didn't simply cover the father's legitimate children and his wife, but all the servants and slaves of the household, as well as, potentially, children fathered with women other than his wife.

It was a picture of extended family that held within it both opportunities and profound limitations. One can imagine that, for some, this structure offered a sense of belonging and safety, shaped around loyalty to the head of the household. In a culture fraught with risk and danger, this family structure offered a wide range of people – not simply those who were blood-related – a sense of being part of a household. On the other hand, members of that household could be at the mercy of a very powerful man (and in some circumstances a very powerful woman). In this form of family, even the designated (male) heir was expected to place his desires and expectations beneath those of the paterfamilias. Equally, weak members of the household were open to the most capricious and cruel exploitation at the hands of the powerful. Legally, dignity within the family was dependent upon the will of the head of the family.

By paying attention to this different understanding of family and household, we may begin to re-read and more fully appreciate some of Jesus' parables and stories. For example, in Luke 9. 29, when the young man comes along and Jesus invites him to follow him and the young man says he must 'bury his father first,' and Jesus is not impressed, this can be puzzling for modern audiences. Why should Jesus be so insensitive about the man's understandable desire to bury his father first? However, if we place this story in a context where the young man is required to show what the Greeks called *pistis* or 'faithful obedience' to his father/paterfamilias in all things, perhaps new possibilities emerge. The young man might be read as saying, 'I must wait until my father is dead, before I can join you.' It might be years before the father dies and frees the son of his obligations!

Equally, understanding the webs of relationships that play out in the cultural context which Jesus negotiated may cast fresh light on classic parables like that of the Lost or Prodigal Son (Luke 15. 11-32). The younger son's request for his share of the property may well have staggered Jesus' original audience in ways we can barely appreciate now. If we and they might both be shocked by the grace shown by the father when he receives his wayward son back, his original audience might have considered the father's original actions as truly bizarre. In a world where a property-owning father could expect unquestioning obedience or disinherit the disobedient heir, the paterfamilias shows a staggering level of indulgence or recklessness in the way he treats the younger son. When we appreciate this, perhaps we may have more sympathy for the disgruntled older son who has shown obedience to his father.

These examples indicate, perhaps, something about Jesus's radicalism. Jesus is less interested in traditional family structures – whether extended, nuclear or whatever – and more interested in faithful commitment to the Living God. As we shall see later in this session, Jesus offers a shocking intervention when his mother and siblings turn up to see him. He asks, 'Who is my mother and brother?' His answer, 'Those who fulfil the will of my father' represents a simultaneous challenge to traditional ideas about family (that some would have found disturbing) and an offer of liberation for those limited by those ideas. Not part of a respectable family household? Don't worry, you can be by following God. Are you an outsider by virtue of your 'blood'/class or job or social standing? Don't worry, God offers you a community of hope. Jesus's radicalism, then, offers new possibilities for those whose experience had been limited by the bounds of 'blood ties', or 'social conventions' (whatever they may be). He reveals new possibilities for family relationships. This can be especially significant for those who've experience family as a place of abuse, violence, exclusion and exploitation.

In the twenty-first century, most people living in the wealthy countries of the Economic North have come to appreciate that the word 'family' can mean many things. We have learnt that the nuclear family is one model within many; equally, we are much less fixated on patriarchal extended family than our forebears. We have seen that family can include same-sex couples and single parents as much as heterosexual couples. Within the Church, we have yet to fully acknowledge the damage done by our idolization of certain so-called 'normal' ideas of what constitute family. Gay couples with children and single parents are still regularly treated as second-class members of the Body of Christ.

Equally, as the horrifying stories of abuse continue to emerge from within faith communities, we see how concepts of the church community as family are open to exploitation by those who wield unregulated power within it.

Nonetheless, as *The Greatest Showman* shows, community and family represents a place for our flourishing and discovering richer truths about ourselves and others. Barnum's family is not simply that of his wife and their children. He discovers ultimately that he is in the hands of others and they in his. The performers in the Circus discover a solidarity, love and respect which is both shaped through their difference from the narrow 'norms' of society and subverts them. They create a new community which is not limited by respectability, blood-ties or class; it is, rather like Jesus' new community, grounded in mutual recognition of the glorious possibility of being human.

PRAYER

Wondrous God, we thank you for your abundant love
    which invites us to find the fullness of life in you.
If we are dust and to dust we shall return,
    help us to know we are fearfully and wonderfully made,
    crowned with glory and honour.
Help us to receive faith, hope and love as gift
    and when we mar your divine image,
    may we hear your voice as you call us back home.
Enable us, through your Spirit, to be people of dreams and visions,
    alert to the call of your Kingdom of Grace and Peace. Amen

Icebreaker
Throughout history, there have been many kinds of family or households. In Britain and modern Christianity since the War, there has often been a bias towards the so-called nuclear family – mum, dad and two or three children. What other kinds of family have you experienced and how have they nourished and encouraged you? Can alternative families set us free from oppressive constraints?

WATCH

The ensemble sings 'Come Alive', watched by their first, sceptical audience (Scene 6, from: 24.20 to 29.27 mins)

In this scene, Barnum has assembled his cast of outsiders and misfits, and prepares to greet a curious, if sceptical, paying crowd for the first time. He sings about how when one is an outsider one is inclined to cast one's head down and expect judgment. He sings, 'I see that lie in your eyes: that you need to hide your face…' Barnum suggests that those who are different must dream with their eyes wide open, but once you start it's impossible to go back into the shadows. As the scene gains momentum, he encourages his debut performers to come out and face the sceptical crowd. Everyone is nervous and a parent in the crowd pushes her daughter away when Lettie Lutz, the bearded lady, appears. Yet, as the cast comes together, confidence is found both within the cast and some of the onlookers, including a disabled boy. However, for all the delight and confidence found, a journalist James Gordon Bennett calls it a primitive circus of humbug and there are threats from people who object.

Think about
In this scene, we see Lettie Lutz, the 'Bearded Lady', anxious about appearing in front of an audience. What do you think she's worried will happen? Where does she find confidence?

The Circus performers come alive as they recognise that they can't go back to the lives they lived before. How difficult can it be to let go of the past and take the risk of living a new life of hope? If you feel confident in the group, share some examples from your own experience.

The new circus community inspires outsiders – including a young lad who uses crutches – but it also attracts the hostility of the critic, James Gordon Bennett, as well as the fear of the New York mob. Why does the circus have these two contrasting effects?

Barnum uses the hostility of Bennett to good effect, offering half-price tickets to anyone who turns up with Bennett's notice 'a primitive circus of humbug'. To what extent is this a good strategy for those on the edge or outside of community to adopt?

GOING DEEPER

Read
Matthew 12:46-50
'Jesus' mother and siblings: Who belongs to Jesus' family?'

As indicated in the opening section of this chapter, in Jesus' time 'family' would have been understood in different ways to those understood in our modern world. Indeed, if we assume that when this passage takes place that Joseph, Jesus' human father, was dead, Jesus would have been the head of the household. Arguably, his behaviour as an itinerant rabbi and preacher might be read as irresponsible. As the head of the household, shouldn't he be looking after his mother and the rest of his extended family? Yet, as we hear in this scene, he doesn't respond to his mother and siblings as either we (a modern audience) or his contemporary audience might expect. He seems to suggest that God – as father of all – is our true 'paterfamilias' or head of household to whom we should offer our faithfulness.

To what extent does this passage disrupt or extend our understandings of 'family' or 'community'?

Is Jesus disrespectful to important ideas about family and God's community, deeply embedded in the Bible?

What hope do Jesus's ideas about 'family' in the Kingdom of Heaven offer to us?

WATCH

The exchange between Bennett and Barnum (From 29.28 to 30.35 mins)

In this short scene, Barnum comes face-to-face with his severest critic, Bennett, the journalist. Bennett challenges Barnum over the authenticity of his 'product'. He asks Barnum if he is concerned that everything he sells is fake. Barnum responds by pointing out that his circus produces real joy. Barnum insists that, 'Men suffer more from imagining too little than too much…' which Bennett considers the creed of a true fraud. Barnum concludes by suggesting that a theatre critic who can't find joy in the theatre is the true fraud.

Think about

We've seen that Barnum has a gift for exaggeration (he overestimates the weight of the world's heaviest man, etc.). Is Bennett correct when he says that everything Barnum offers is fake? If not, what does he have a gift for offering?

Perhaps Barnum has a gift for creating a show that helps the circus members and the audience experience something greater than themselves. What are the benefits and risks of that gift?

Barnum says that humanity suffers more from imagining too little than too much. Do you agree or disagree? If so, why?

Are there generational differences? Increasingly it

is claimed that young people have been encouraged to dream and find it difficult when faced with the humdrum. Do you agree?

GOING DEEPER

Read
Matthew 13:10-16
'Why parables?'

This scene takes place after Jesus has told one of his most famous parables, the story of the sower and the seed. It dares to ask why Jesus speaks in stories. It is of interest in the context of a discussion of Barnum because Barnum is accused of making things up and tricking people. Yet, as we see with Jesus, sometimes storytelling and fantasy can be a way of revealing the truth.

In Matthew 13, Jesus seems to imply that stories reveal as well as conceal the truth; that not everyone will hear the truth contained within them. Do you agree?

In her *Harry Potter* novels, J. K. Rowling suggests that words are 'our most powerful form of magic.' How plausible do you find this claim?

The fantasy writer Neil Gaiman claims that 'Fairytales are more than true, not because they tell us that dragons exist, but because they tell us dragons can be defeated.' To what extent do both Barnum and Jesus deploy stories which reflect that dictum?

To what extent do parables and stories help us to live up to the Christian Way? Offer examples from your own life of the impact of parables on your Christian pilgrimage.

WATCH

Caroline dances in the ballet, and is snubbed by the privileged young ladies (From: 31.48 to 34.09 mins)

Earlier in the film, when asked to make a wish, one of Barnum's daughters, Caroline, asks for ballet shoes. After Barnum achieves success and moves into the home he and Charity dreamt of as children, Caroline receives those shoes and begins to dance. She ends up dancing with girls from high society and receives a quite devastating snub from these snobby young ladies. His daughter decides to quit, saying 'I started too late.' When Barnum tries to encourage her, she says, 'It's not like the circus … you can't just fake it.'

Think about

What do we make of the response of the wealthy girls to Caroline? Have you ever experienced anything like that? Have you ever behaved like that to anyone else?

Have you ever quit or been tempted to quit something because you faced opposition?

Have you ever attempted to make yourself more respectable to fit in with a dominant group? What do we risk when we seek to fit in? What might we gain?

GOING DEEPER

Read
Matthew 9:10-17
'Jesus Eats with Tax-Collectors and Sinners'

Having called the tax-collector Matthew to follow him, Jesus eats with a host of unrespectable people. Despite the reasonable concerns that he is being unrighteous for doing do, Jesus persists and defends his actions.

Unlike the characters in the ballet scene, Jesus seems unaffected by the rules of social distinction and cultural appropriateness. Indeed, Jesus is accused of being unrespectable and unrighteous. What does his behaviour reveal about God's priorities?

How easy is it to be faithful to Jesus' way?

Do we count ourselves among the righteous or the unrighteous? How is God challenging us?

WATCH

Barnum and Carlyle sing 'To the Other Side' in which Barnum tries to persuade rakish playwright Carlyle to join the Circus (From: 34.10 to 39.19 mins)

In this scene, Barnum attempts to recruit wealthy, High Society playwright Philip Carlyle to his cause. Carlyle is handsome, well-connected and rich, if a bit of an *enfant terrible*. He has had a successful play performed in London. Barnum senses that Carlyle might offer him a route into High Society and respectability. Carlyle – who feels trapped by his gilded lifestyle – senses the pull of circus life, but also knows it will potentially cost him his status and inheritance. He says he's okay with the 'uptown' part he gets to play and is worried he'll become just another clown. Yet, Carlyle longs for freedom from his constrained life.

Think about

Carlyle has a comfortable and pleasant life – one that would have been extremely rare in the rough world of nineteenth-century New York. Is he foolish for risking it all by associating with Barnum? What does he stand to gain?

Have we ever felt stifled by the lives we lead? The song talks about 'the other side' – for Barnum this is respectability, for Carlyle this is risk, excitement and danger. What is it about humans that we often think the grass is greener on the other side?

Have we ever taken risks for the sake of finding a better or richer life? How did that feel? If we haven't, why not?

GOING DEEPER

Read
Mark 10:17-31 (If you are pressed for time, read Mark 10. 29-31)
'The Rich and the Kingdom of God'

This reading focuses on one of Jesus' encounters on the road, this time with a wealthy young man. This is someone who seeks to fulfil the Law and be a good and holy person. Yet, when faced with Jesus' answer to the question, 'What must I do to inherit eternal life?', he is broken by its final clause: 'Go, sell what you own and give it to the poor.'

In some respects, the character of Carlyle is like that of the wealthy young man. Perhaps many of us in a wealthy country like the United Kingdom can be counted among the wealthy too. Jesus says, 'Go, sell what you own and give the money to the poor and you will have treasure in heaven.' How challenging do we find Jesus's words? What are the 'attachments' we have that prevent us from having more abundant life?

Jesus promises abundant life – in this world and the next – for those who take the risk of following him with everything they have. What are the signs of abundant life in your own life, if any?

How much of life do we spend trying to make life secure? What do we risk losing if we follow Jesus wholeheartedly?

LOOKING AHEAD... ACTIVITIES TO CONSIDER THIS WEEK

In his book, *The God of Surprises* (London: DLT, 2008), Gerard W. Hughes explores how the prayer practices of St Ignatius of Loyola can help us discern the way to follow Jesus more clearly in our lives. He shows how St Ignatius' exercises help us discern the things which get in the way of following Christ more completely and let them go. Ignatius calls them 'attachments' and they can take many forms, from excessive love of material things, or security or self-obsession and vanity. This week, consider getting hold of Hughes' book and try praying some of Ignatius' exercises. (To find out more about the prayer exercises of St Ignatius, resources can be found on the internet. See, for example: https://www.ignatianspirituality.com/ignatian-prayer/the-spiritual-exercises/an-ignatian-prayer-adventure)

Alternatively, consider offering prayer this week for the many kinds of family found in our society. How can you become supportive of those who have traditionally been excluded by the Church's focus on heterosexual, nuclear families? How can you encourage your church or faith community to celebrate the varieties of family life (including those people whose family or household consists of themselves alone)?

CLOSING PRAYER

Scandalous God,
You choose the way of foolishness.
As you dwell with us in vulnerability,
*   help us to discover riches in your poverty*
*   and poverty in our riches.*
Guide and encourage us along your Way of hope,
*   and disturb our complacency,*
*   that we may dare follow you into new life. Amen*

(A version of this prayer was originally published in my book *A Star-Filled Grace: Worship and Prayer Resources for Advent, Christmas and Epiphany* (Glasgow: Wild Goose, 2015).

WEEK 3

'Rewrite the Stars'

TO START YOU THINKING

'Jesus said to them, "Give to the emperor the things that are the emperor's, and to God the things that are God's." ' (Mark 12. 17)

About thirty years ago, I went on a camping and hiking holiday with a friend in Scotland. We were young students and I think it's fair to say that I liked to dress like what we called 'a bit of crusty'. In short, I had dreadlocks and wore grubby, casual clothes. My friend and I set off with the typical enthusiasm of the young and were soon to encounter the small 'c' conservatism of some rural Scottish communities. As we walked through a pretty village on a hot day, we passed a charming family-run hotel. We were both thirsty and fancied a drink so I volunteered to step inside and see if we could buy one. I found the proprietor and, in my politest voice, said, 'Excuse me, are you open to non-residents?' She looked me up and down and said, 'Not to the likes of you we're not.' At the time, I was both irritated and quite amused. Before I left the hotel, I said, 'Jesus didn't wear a suit, you know.'

That moment in a Scottish hotel, was a powerful encounter with respectability. Looking back, even if I disagree with the landlady's response to me, I find it more understandable. As I've got older I've become more respectable and conservative. Even if I seek to maintain my own distinctive style, it is very much 'respectable'.

I don't know if we all become more conventional with age, but I know that I no longer need to show off in the way I did as a teenager. As a parish priest, I've had to learn which lines one can comfortably cross and those that present more of a challenge to one's parishioners.

This week's session explores how *The Greatest Showman* opens-up ways for us to reflect on the temptations to prioritise respectability over faithfulness to what we truly believe in. We see how Barnum, who has found success by sticking with outsiders and doing things differently, begins to desire the praise of middle-class respectable people. He is tempted to betray those with whom he has become friends – his circus – by seeking affirmation among the great and the good. We also witness how the respectably-born Carlyle is prepared to take the risk of becoming the partner of Anne Wheeler, an African-American. Their 'mixed-race' relationship is, contextually, a profound challenge to the racist culture of mid-nineteenth-century America.

These themes open-up the possibility of exploring how Jesus' unrespectable ministry can be read as challenging the respectability and righteous of his day. Jesus' centre of value is always God. It remains as much a challenge to us today as it did to his first audiences. In the Gospels, we see him challenging, again and again, both his disciples and his auditors, among whom included members of the Pharisee and Sadducee groups, as well as those whom he heals.

It has become something of a lazy trope to cast some of Jesus' audience as the arch-representatives of respectability and righteousness. So, the Sadducees – a group primarily associated with the ruling class in Judea, and also sometimes associated with the Herodian party – have been treated as agents of respectability. The Pharisees – a theologically reforming group in Judaism – have often been portrayed as examples not only of respectability, but of 'self-righteousness', more concerned with the outward demonstration of loyalty to the Law rather than inner faith. Both have acted as stereotypes for Judaism and Jewish people more broadly. The Pharisees have often been treated as stand-ins for Jews and spurs to Anti-Semitic attitudes.

The scene in Mark 12:13-17 (from which the headline quote of this chapter is taken) reveals a great deal about how Jesus' 'opponents' were stereotyped by the Gospel writers. In it, we witness a delegation of Herodians and Pharisees who come before Jesus to 'trap him in what he said'. They wish to know whether it is lawful to pay taxes to the Emperor or not. Jesus gives a typically brilliant response, inviting them to answer their own question by asking whose image is found on the coins they hold. He concludes, 'Give to the emperor the things that are the emperor's, and to God the things that are God's.' What is striking is how Jesus' interlocutors are presented as cunning and sly and already conspiring against him. They are presented as agents of the status quo who will use any means to trick Jesus.

It may come as a shock, but recent scholarship is inclined to be critical of the traditional association in Christianity between 'Pharisee' and 'Sadducee' and wickedness. Indeed, it has been suggested that Jesus himself was probably closely allied to the Pharisee party, and many of his critical and creative readings (or 'midrash') of the Law and the Prophets were allied to the reforming Pharisee spirit. If Jesus wasn't close to the Pharisees, it is surely surprising that so many hang around him pretty much from the outset of his ministry. It may surprise you that the Pharisees who have come to be associated with a kind of priggish adherence to Law over grace, were imaginative and creative people who were searching for ways to be faithful to God. For them, as much as for Jesus – a faithful and committed Jew – the Law was not a burden but a gift of grace. It was a sign of blessing.

What is the case is that the Gospel indicates that Jesus had a gift for going too far for many in his community. His focus on God led him to alienate some people who were unconvinced by Jesus' reasoning or saw in him a profound threat to the uneasy settlement between the Jewish establishment and the Roman occupiers. Judea was seen by many Romans as the 'back-end' of the Empire, always on the edge of rebellion and violence. Jesus' questing, dangerous call to be faithful to the Living God, made figures across the theological and political spectrum nervous. Jesus was – from the evidence of the Gospels – seen as a respected, if risky Rabbi, but his desire to always place God's call centre-stage was by turns too radical and too risky for many. Jesus was no hot-head. His handling of the incident just described proved that. He was quite capable of offering clever answers to dangerous questions. Yet, he was also capable of overturning tables in the Temple and challenging his audiences, as in the parable of the Good Samaritan, to see outsiders and othered people as neighbours.

In this week's study, we see how much Barnum is like us, rather than like Jesus. His head is easily turned towards respectability and fitting in with the status quo rather than challenging it. He wants the goods of middle-class society to be his. Equally, we explore the costs of breaking those middle-class rules through the story of Anne Wheeler and Carlyle. Carlyle has risked everything to join the circus and he falls in love with Anne. He thinks that together they can 'rewrite the stars' and break free of a society that shows prejudice based on the colour of a person's skin. Anne is more realistic and thinks their love is doomed. Ultimately, this week's session explores the serious challenges to our vocation to follow Jesus that are still faced by many in the modern world. Indeed, if the world in which we lived has changed much since Jesus' day and since the setting of *The Greatest Showman*, the call to be faithful to the Way of justice and truth remains as fraught as it ever did.

OPENING PRAYER

Wondrous God, we thank you for your abundant love
    which invites us to find the fullness of life in you.
If we are dust and to dust we shall return,
    help us to know we are fearfully and wonderfully
    made,
    crowned with glory and honour.
Help us to receive faith, hope and love as gift
    and when we mar your divine image,
    may we hear your voice as you call us back home.
Enable us, through your Spirit, to be people of dreams
    and visions,
    alert to the call of your Kingdom of Grace and
    Peace. Amen

Icebreaker

What kind of barriers, if any, have you experienced in your life? To what extent have you experienced being treated differently, perhaps because of gender, class, skin colour, disability or sexuality? Perhaps, even because of faith? How have you dealt with these kinds of experiences?

WATCH

Barnum is reminded of the opposition to his dream and receives an unexpected invitation into the highest society possible (From: 39.44 to 42.47 mins)

As Barnum and his team go from strength to strength, he is reminded of the growing opposition to him, not only from violent elements in society, but from the respectable 'pen' of Bennett the journalist. As Barnum ever more wants to be accepted by society, he begins to doubt whether controversy is enough. Carlyle comes up with an unexpected invitation to visit Queen Victoria at Buckingham Palace. However, Anne Wheeler flags up the circus's anxiety that not everyone will be invited. Carlyle says, 'either all of us go or none of us.' At Queen Victoria's court, the circus is met with suspicion, but General Tom Thumb – who has truly found his sassy voice – causes a sensation when he breaks with Royal protocol and makes Victoria laugh.

Think about

To what extent are Barnum's anxieties sensible ones? Has he become too seduced by the desire for respectability and position?

What do you make of the challenge made by Anne Wheeler to Carlyle ('Are we all invited?')? Is it a wake-up call to Carlyle's assumptions? When have we received such jolts to our comfortable ideas?

Have any of us, like Tom Thumb, ever broken accepted protocols with unexpected results? How did it feel? Were there repercussions?

GOING DEEPER

Read
Luke 9:46-48
'The Greatest in the Kingdom'

This is one of the most famous sections of the gospels, in which Jesus challenges our desire for position and respectability. He suggests that it is not being powerful or wealthy or high-status that matters, but 'being the least'. Arguably, it speaks powerfully into Barnum's aspirations, as well as many of ours. How challenging do you find this claim? Why?

T. S. Eliot claimed that, 'One of the most deadening influences upon the Church in the past ... was its acceptance, by the upper, upper middle and aspiring classes, as a political necessity and as a requirement of respectability ...' Writing in the 1930s he said that, because of shifts in politics, literature and culture, 'the orthodox faith of England is at last relieved from its burden of respectability.' How do you respond to Eliot's claim? Does it apply even more today or are Christians tempted to prioritise respectability over their faith?

What might your church look like if it took Jesus's words about the greatest seriously?

WATCH

Carlyle's first encounter with Anne Wheeler (Re-watch from 38.59 to 39.45 mins) as well as Carlyle's visit to the theatre with Anne where they meet Carlyle's parents (From 58.57 to 1.01.01 mins)

In the first of these two scenes, we witness Carlyle's first encounter with the trapeze artist Anne Wheeler (and her brother W.D.) and see the class and ethnic suspicions between a man of privilege and a couple who face daily prejudice (earlier in the film, we heard W.D. say that people would not be happy about seeing them on stage). In the second scene, we see the effects of prejudice first-hand. Anne attends the theatre and, in the company of Carlyle, bumps into Carlyle's parents. They are doubly-ashamed of their son. Firstly, he has demeaned the family name by associating with a circus and, secondly, he is seen out with (in Carlyle's father's words) 'the help'. Carlyle is furious with his parents and tells Anne that they are small-minded people to be ignored. She says in response, 'you've never had someone look at you the way your parents looked at me'.

Think about

How does the reaction of Carlyle's parents to Anne make you feel? What do you think of the reaction of Anne and of Carlyle?

The Greatest Showman is set in the mid-nineteenth-century United States. Slavery was still legal, if generally disapproved of in New York where the film is set. There were still high levels of prejudice and discrimination even in non-slave states. Does this excuse the reactions of Carlyle's parents?

Carlyle's parents represent respectability and authority. In their historical context, their views were of a piece with US conventional white middle-class Christianity. What are the views we hold that might be open to question in years to come, by future generations?

GOING DEEPER

Read
Acts 10:9-23
'Peter's vision'

This passage includes Peter's famous vision of 'unclean' food. The context for this vision is, broadly, the spread of the early Christian faith beyond the disciples and Jewish people to include gentiles. Specifically, the context concerns Cornelius, a Roman soldier who is described as 'a devout man who feared God with all his household'. This indicates that he someone who respects Jewish traditions, but is not a Jewish convert. He receives a vision to invite Peter to come into his household. Peter is disinclined to come, but receives a vision himself, of being invited to eat ritually impure or unclean food. God tells him that what God has made pure he should not call unclean. It is a vision which ultimately breaks down Peter's resistance to new possibilities of faith and leads him to come to Cornelius's house and say, 'I truly understand that God shows no partiality, but in every nation anyone who fears him and does what is right is acceptable to him.'

How shocking might it have been for Peter to receive

this challenge to his ideas about righteous and holy behaviour? Why?

Have any of us ever experienced challenges from God (or wider society) to rethink our ideas about what is 'respectable', 'righteous' or 'holy'? If you have share examples.

What are the places of challenge in modern faith and Christianity?

WATCH

Carlyle and Anne Wheeler sing 'Rewrite the Stars' (From: 1.01.01 to 1.04.36 mins)

In this scene, the 'star-crossed' lovers Carlyle and Anne sing about rewriting the stars. Carlyle believes it's possible, but, as Anne demonstrates her death-defying skills, she reveals how difficult it is for them to be together outside of the 'walls' of the circus. As they perform together they learn new levels of trust and refuse to accept the limits society places on their relationship. They take risks together, but Anne concludes that outside of the power she has claimed in the circus they cannot be together.

Think about

Anne and Carlyle are caught between a vision of what might be (Carlyle) and realism (Anne). Who in your view is closer to the truth? Why?

The circus ring has become a safe place for Anne and Carlyle to express their love. How important are safe spaces for those who don't fit society's norms. What are modern equivalents?

At the heart of making the trapeze successful is trust and practice. The lovers sing, 'All I want is to fly with you … all I want is to fall with you.' Might this be a good image for our relationships with our loved ones and most especially with God?

In a prejudiced world, how can we help 'Rewrite the Stars' and challenge injustice?

GOING DEEPER

Read
Hebrews 11:1-3, 8-16
'The Risk of Faith'

The whole of Hebrews Chapter 11 is about faith and risk and – in a quiet moment – is worth meditating on. The writer of the Letter of the Hebrews is determined to indicate how everything in biblical history and the history of the world points towards the salvation in Jesus Christ. S/he reminds us that figures like Abraham and Sarah sought to live on God's promises even when they had no idea where their trust in God would lead them. God is faithful to those who seek to be faithful to him, even those who – like Abraham, Moses and the prophets – had no prospect of seeing the salvation in Jesus Christ in their lifetimes.

Carlyle and Anne are tempted to abandon their love in the face of societal and cultural prejudices. In what ways, if any, does this passage encourage us not to give up, even when we think that our respectable and prejudiced world impedes God's work?

How has God called you 'out of yourself' into believing or accepting something new? How has your understanding of the Gospel shifted over time?

What sign of God's Kingdom of Love do you think will only be revealed after you have died?

WATCH

Tensions spill over and the theatre is destroyed by bigots
(From: 1.11.47 to 1.15.55 mins)

In this scene, Carlyle is threatened by bigoted thugs who want the Circus to close, and Anne's brother W.D. stands by him. There is a fight which brings in the whole of the circus, and the theatre is burned down. Carlyle goes back in to rescue Anne, but is trapped. Barnum, recently returned from his tour with Jenny Lind, rescues Carlyle and we see Anne waiting at his bedside as she sings a reprise of 'rewrite the stars'.

Think about
The thugs want Carlyle and the Circus to leave town. How commendable is his, W.D. and the entire circus's response to the threats? Why do you think that?

When Carlyle and W.D. are threatened, the Circus respond as one body. They show 'corporate solidarity' – a standing-by each other. Do you think the circus's response to the threats offers a model for modern resistance to bullying and threats?

What might a 'Christian response' to the thugs look like? Would it involve violence and active resistance?

GOING DEEPER

Read
James 1: 2-8, 19-27
'The Faith Community Under Pressure'

This letter represents a powerful shout-out of
encouragement to an early Christian community
under pressure. They face temptation from the world
to conform to its ways and are under pressure to give
up their faith. This suggests it was written to an early
community that may have included Jews under pressure
to revert to older traditions or Greeks who were under
pressure to fit in with the wider pagan culture.

In the opening section, James writes, 'My brothers
and sisters, whenever you face trials of any kind, consider
it nothing but joy, because you know that the testing of
your faith produces endurance; and let endurance have
its full effect, so that you may be mature and complete,
lacking in nothing.' What are the trials we can face?
Does this passage encourage or irritate us?

When James writes, 'You must understand this, my
beloved: let everyone be quick to listen, slow to speak,
slow to anger; for your anger does not produce God's
righteousness' is he helpful in our faith journeys? Do
these words apply when we face huge prejudice as the
circus does in *The Greatest Showman*?

If this passage represents a Christian response to
trial, setbacks and suffering, what would our living it out
in church and the world look like?

LOOKING AHEAD... ACTIVITIES TO CONSIDER THIS WEEK

In recent years, there have been many campaigns which aim to address prejudice in society. Many of these have taken off online on social media, including the #metoo, #blacklivesmatter and #everydaysexism campaigns. If you haven't heard of them, take some time to investigate them and see how you can get involved.

Consider joining a campaigning organisation like *Amnesty International* which seeks human rights across the globe. If you are already a member, get involved in their latest campaign. Christian Aid, Cafod and Tearfund, among others, offer ways to engage with justice issues across the world. Consider donating or signing up to their campaigning work.

Equally, you might seek to address injustices in your church or local context. If you are not already a member, speak to your vicar or church wardens about joining Inclusive Church; if your church is already a member, is it time to revisit your commitments and investigate how you can take inclusion to the next level? For more info, see: https://www.inclusive-church.org

CLOSING PRAYER

Righteous God,
You dare to turn over the tables of injustice
     and show your love to those on the margins.
Help us to respond to your call with delight and trust,
     that we may show your passion for a world in need.
Through your Spirit, grant us faith and courage
     to follow the Way of your son, Jesus Christ. Amen

WEEK 4

'Never Enough'

TO START YOU THINKING

The late medieval world took betrayal very seriously. One indication of this is found Dante Alighieri's *Inferno*, the opening part of his magnificent *Divine Comedy*. As Dante is guided by Virgil through the nine circles of hell and witnesses the fate of those who've been guilty of specific sins (lust, gluttony and so on), he finally arrives at the lowest circle. In it are just three figures. Firstly, there is Cassius and Brutus. They, of course, are famously the betrayers of Julius Caesar. In Shakespeare's play of the same name, Caesar says, 'Et tu, Brute?' meaning 'Even you, Brutus?' Finally, there is Judas Iscariot. He is treated as the very lowest of the low because he has betrayed the very Son of God.

In the modern world, we are perhaps inclined to be a little more generous to the likes of Judas. Since at least the early 1960s, there has been a renewed interest in him. In Nicholas Ray's 1961 epic *King of Kings*, Rip Torn portrays Judas as a passionate freedom fighter for an occupied Judea, who betrays Jesus to force his hand. In the immensely successful 1970s' musical *Jesus Christ Superstar*, Judas is humanised and seen as someone who wants the best for his occupied people. He is shown as someone who loves Jesus, as much as he is frightened by him. When he sings 'Heaven on their Minds', Rice and Lloyd Webber imbue Judas with human fear and doubt, and we can even sympathise with his willingness to betray his friend for the sake of saving his nation and himself. In that musical, Judas is much more like us, and – arguably – more sympathetic than Jesus.

Equally, in theology, W. H. Vanstone, the great Anglican parish priest and spiritual director, wrote a book called *The Stature of Waiting* which helps us re-read Judas. It examines, in part, the nature of Judas's betrayal of Jesus and Vanstone indicates that the word used for betrayal in the Gospels means 'handed-over'. It creates a different sense to Judas's action, removing some of the moral censure associated with betrayal. Vanstone explores how, in handing Jesus over to his fate, Judas is a participant in God's work of salvation: that, as Jesus embraces being handed over to his torturers and killers, Judas reveals how God saves us.

In recent times, Susan Gubar, the well-known feminist literary scholar, has explored Judas's place in Christian history and tradition in her book *Judas: A Biography*. While it doesn't pretend to reveal the full human story of Judas – the evidence is too thin to write a biography in the traditional sense – she reveals how much he has been the whipping boy in Christian tradition. He has been used and abused to represent everything from Christian prejudices about Jewish people to those about gay people. Indeed, she reveals how Judas – the great betrayer and 'money grubber' – has been used to bolster Anti-Semitism and justify the vilest treatment and stereotypes of Jewish people.

We might like to believe that we are above the sin of betrayal, but I'm not so sure. It can take a variety of forms. Sometimes it's signalled in what we fail to do as much as in what we do. Thus, sometimes when people think about World War Two they ask, why did people occupied by the Nazis collaborate or fail to resist? Why didn't more Germans or Poles stand up for the Jews? It's easy for people in the UK to think we wouldn't have fallen in line and might have protected our Jewish or gay friends. The reality would have been more complex.

It would have taken few active collaborators to have denuded North Manchester or North London of its Jewish populations; it would have taken a lot of passive people turning their eyes the other way for the crime to have been completed. To turn away is arguably a form of betrayal too.

If that is a high-level example far removed from our everyday experience, perhaps we have all committed lower-level and everyday betrayals. I remember, when I was a teenager, how embarrassed I was about my friends meeting my parents or certain aunts. I felt like I wanted to keep my friends away from family and vice versa, in case it reflected badly on me (who wanted to be liked by friends). It seems silly now, but at the time it really mattered. To snub my family – with whom I had important and deep obligations and relationships – for the sake of my friends, was arguably a form of betrayal. On other occasions, I'm ashamed to admit I dropped one or two friends in those years because they didn't fit my image of myself.

Jesus is betrayed, as the Gospel of Matthew has it, by a friend and disciple for money. I hope that this introductory section has helped us recognise that Judas is a subtler figure than we sometimes think. Nonetheless, Matthew indicates that Judas is motivated by venal desires. Every one of us knows what it is to let people down or fail to act as fully for the good as we might. If we are not exactly like Judas, we are all corruptible and can prioritise our love of money or position or power over goodness and God.

In this week's session, we witness how Barnum's desire to be popular and respectable leads him to betray what he most believes in: his family and his friends. He has his head turned by the possibilities opened up by the opera singer, Jenny Lind, the 'Swedish Nightingale'. Barnum has already received more than enough – in terms of money, blessings, and the good life – by the time

Lind appears, but he refuses to be satisfied. He wants more, most especially position and respect from those who are higher up in society. It places him in a parlous situation where he might end up losing everything. As he turns towards the glamour of the high life, he turns his back on what is real. He begins to betray those who truly love and respect him. It is a deeply human story and one with which almost all of us can identify. We may not be exactly like Judas, but we too have to face our betrayals and pray that we receive sufficient grace to find a way back to the good.

OPENING PRAYER

Wondrous God, we thank you for your abundant love
    which invites us to find the fullness of life in you.
If we are dust and to dust we shall return,
    help us to know we are fearfully and wonderfully
    made,
    crowned with glory and honour.
Help us to receive faith, hope and love as gift
    and when we mar your divine image,
    may we hear your voice as you call us back home.
Enable us, through your Spirit, to be people of dreams
    and visions,
    alert to the call of your Kingdom of Grace and
    Peace. Amen

Icebreaker

How difficult is it to remain faithful to our principles or commitments? In your opinion, is it more admirable to be prepared to compromise or to stick to your beliefs? Have you ever compromised to get something you wanted for yourselves or others?

WATCH

Barnum's first encounter with the world's greatest soprano, Miss Jenny Lind and her debut in New York (From: 42.50 to 51.00 mins)

In this scene, Barnum meets the greatest singer in Europe, the 'Swedish Nightingale' Jenny Lind. He says he wants to offer people something authentic for once, rather than hoodwink people. However, on the night of Lind's performance, the circus turns up to watch. Barnum tells Carlyle to put them in the standing area, the cheap section, rather than have them in the box. Meanwhile all of New York's respectable people, including Carlyle's and Charity's parents turn up. Lind sings and is a sensation. Even the cynical journalist Bennett gives her a standing ovation.

Think about
Barnum says that he wants to offer people something real for once. To what extent is that his real motivation?

What is your response to Barnum's treatment of the circus members? To what extent does he betray them by putting them in the standing area? Is he cruel when he implies they are a side-show, when he introduces Jenny Lind?

Would you be tempted, like Barnum, to betray your past and commitments if it meant you could be given something you've deeply longed for?

Barnum 'drops' his old friends from the circus for

new more glamorous ones. Why? Have you ever done anything similar (perhaps when you wanted to be popular as a teenager or when you were feeling insecure)?

GOING DEEPER

Read
Hebrews 4:14-16
'Our Great High Priest'

In this passage from the Letter to the Hebrews, we read of Jesus Christ as a 'great high priest' who has been tempted in every way, but is without sin. The implication is that he has faced every temptation, including our temptation to betray, and yet has passed the test. In doing so, it is suggested that we can trust in him and approach the 'the throne of grace' with boldness. In short, because he has never betrayed God or others or himself (for he has been faithful), we can trust him never to betray us.

Does Jesus run the risk of being too perfect and unrelatable? If yes, why is that? If not, why not?

Is Barnum a much more relatable character because he knows what it is to sin?

The writer of Hebrews says, 'We do not have a high priest who is unable to sympathize with our weaknesses, but we have one who in every respect has been tested as we are, yet without sin.' How helpful is this claim as you negotiate the ups and downs of your faith?

The writer then goes on to say, 'Let us therefore approach the throne of grace with boldness, so that we may receive mercy and find grace to help in time of need.' If you are able, talk about occasions when Jesus has helped you find grace in a time of need, especially in the face of temptation.

WATCH

At the reception for Jenny Lind (From: 51.00 to 54.07 mins (just before 'This is Me'))

At the reception for Jenny Lind, all New York high society turns up, including Charity's parents, Mr and Mrs Hallett. Her father says that Barnum has done well. Barnum reacts out of his anger and tells the Halletts to get out. Charity is angry. Jenny toasts Barnum and says that he shows that a man's station is only limited by his imagination, and Barnum is flattered. The circus performers then appear and Barnum shuts them out. Lettie Lutz is shattered and humiliated by Barnum's behaviour.

Think about

To what extent is Barnum's reaction to Mr Hallett understandable?

How manipulative is Jenny Lind when she flatters Barnum, or does she have a point that a person's station in life is only limited by their imagination? Is Lind speaking out of a position of privilege?

What do you make of Barnum's behaviour around the circus performers? How okay is it? How might you feel if you were in the position of Lettie Lutz and the others?

Have you ever experienced being snubbed? If you feel safe to do so, reflect on the experience. What was it like?

Does Barnum reveal himself to be more like Judas than Jesus in this scene? What is he betraying?

WATCH

Lettie Lutz and the ensemble's response to Barnum's betrayal … 'This is me!' (From: 54.07 to 57.46 mins)

In this scene, Lettie sings about resisting the view that she is nothing. Indeed, she says that those who are different are glorious. She leads the people of the Circus away from Barnum's reception into the theatre and claims space for herself and others. Tom Thumb joins in and the circus runs the gauntlet of hate from those outside the theatre. Together they find strength and community.

Think about
What do you make of the circus's response to a betrayal of trust?

It suggests that community/family forged out of adversity is much more powerful than community forged out of privilege. How plausible do you find this? Can you find examples from the modern world to support it?

Does this response have anything to teach us about being faithful to ourselves and our beliefs when we are let down by those whom we trust?

GOING DEEPER

Read
Matthew 26:6-16
'Jesus anointed at Bethany'

In this scene, we see a contrast between the faithful love of an outsider, a woman, who is mocked for her extravagance, and the readiness of Judas, the insider, to betray his friend and master for money.

What do you make of this scene from the Gospels when placed alongside the scenes we've just watched from *The Greatest Showman*?

What are the temptations you face which might lead you away from being faithful to God, or truth or ethical behaviour?

How do you see Judas? Do you think he's been unfairly treated by Christian tradition? To what extent is he a convenient scapegoat for us?

Barnum goes on tour with Jenny and, to make a profit, Jenny has to perform dozens of times. The time apart places enormous strain on Barnum's relationship with Charity and his family. When Barnum leaves home to go on tour, Charity tells him that we don't need to be loved by everyone, just by a few good people. How far do you agree with Charity? Why?

WATCH

The moment of decision … (From: 1.08.42 to 1.11.44 mins)

While on tour, Barnum comes to a moment of decision. Jenny says they have the world at their feet and they nearly kiss. 'I've given you the world', says Jenny, but Barnum decides to resist the temptation. Barnum needs Jenny to finish the tour to save him from ruin. Jenny is arguably betrayed by Barnum and strikes back by kissing him on stage.

Think about
With whom do you have more sympathy? Jenny or Barnum?

How admirable is Barnum's decision to resist temptation, given the fact he left Charity and the girls behind?

Does Barnum deserve to be ruined? Give reasons for your view.

GOING DEEPER

Read
Mark 8:34-37
'What will it profit them …'

This is justly one of the most famous readings in the

Gospels. It indicates not only the cost of following Jesus and his invitation to take up the Cross, but outlines the risks of mistaking the goods of this world for the gifts of God.

Jesus says, 'For what will it profit them to gain the whole world and forfeit their life?' How much does this statement apply to Barnum?

What resonances does this verse have in your Christian journey?

Can you give any examples of when you or others have failed to resist the temptation to put your soul at risk? How did you respond to this situation? What 'saved' you, if anything?

WATCH

Barnum's encounter with the theatre critic Bennett outside the burned-out theatre (From: 1:15.57 to 1:18.50)

Barnum sits in the rubble of the theatre and his life. Bennett appears and shows him a newspaper that reveals that Jenny Lind kissed him and that she has quit the tour. Barnum rushes off to explain to Charity, only to find she already knows and has decided to leave him. Barnum discovers that their house is also about to be repossessed. Charity says, 'I never minded the risk but we always did it together…' and leaves. Barnum's world has gone up in flames and he reaches his lowest point.

Think about
What do you make of Bennett's claim that 'putting all peoples, of all colours … on stage together… some people might even have called it a celebration of humanity…'?

How reasonable and admirable is Charity's response to Barnum's behaviour?

Barnum's life is in ruins. What is his abiding sin?

What is/are the lesson/s he needs to learn?

What can we learn from Barnum's fall from grace?

GOING DEEPER

Read
Job 1:1-22
'The blameless man loses everything'

The Book of Job is a mythic account of faithfulness
and suffering. Job is a blameless and upright man who
loses everything. The set-up includes Satan – who is not
necessarily to be treated as equivalent to the devil of
Christian tradition, but is here a rather puckish 'heavenly
being' – suggesting to God that Job's righteousness
reflects his privilege. In short, Job has everything and
has never truly been put to the test. So, God permits
Satan to take all Job's privilege and power away from
him to see how Job reacts.

In what ways might Barnum and Job's positions be
similar? How are they different?

If the set-up for Job's suffering is (as the theologian
Trevor Dennis suggests in *Face to Face With God:
Moses, Eluma and Job*, London, SPCK, 1999) a little
pantomime, the reality of Job's suffering is not. Job's
response is not to blame God (even later in the book,
when his so-called friends tell him to blame God). What
are the situations you have faced where you have lost
power, privilege or safety? How did you react?

Is it unreasonable to blame God for bad things that
happen to good people? If it is, why? If not, what can we
say to someone who has experienced bad things they did
not deserve?

LOOKING AHEAD... ACTIVITIES TO CONSIDER THIS WEEK

It can be very difficult for us to live well in a consumerist world. We are surrounded by temptations to buy things we don't need or put our selfish interests first. Even when we buy necessities, often it's difficult to do so without exploiting other people. Those of us who live in countries like the UK, have become used to cheap consumer goods produced by people working in other parts of the world. Arguably, when we act in an unthinking way with our money, resources and stewardship, we are betraying our sisters and brothers in other parts of the world.

So, this week, explore how you can be more responsible with your resources. Can you replace non-fairly-traded goods with those which are? Where practicable and finances allow, be alert to how you use your finances. Can you donate to your local food bank? In a time when dis-proportionate resources are used to raise cheap meat, try going vegetarian or even vegan for a week.

As a longer-term project, explore with others how your church can become an 'eco-church'. For more information, see: https://ecochurch.arocha.org.uk

CLOSING PRAYER

Generous God,
When we fall from grace,
    you wait for us and call us back home.
Help us to listen to your invitation
    to turn back around to face your love
    and dare to seek your forgiveness.
Guide and encourage us along your Way of hope,
    and disturb our complacency,
    that, boldly, we may follow you into new life. Amen

WEEK 5

'From Now On'

TO START YOU THINKING

'… being found in human form,
he humbled himself
and became obedient to the point of death—
even death on a cross.' (Philippians 2:7-8)

When I was in my mid-twenties I had a quite overwhelming religious experience. Having rejected Christianity in my teens, as I entered my twenties, I slowly felt drawn back towards God and prayer. Then, at Whitsun 1996, I got down on my knees and prayed, 'God, if you are there, then I am yours.' To my utter, overwhelming shock, God was. It marked for me, a moment when I definitely began to return to God.

In this final week of study, we explore various ideas about redemption. The story I've told above, represents one picture of what redemption in the Christian tradition looks like. It is a picture of someone encountering God in such a way that their life is renewed and recreated and turned-around. Quite often, that renewal is predicated on a strong experience of forgiveness. Thus, one approaches God with a deep sense of inadequacy, brokenness or, in traditional language, of sin. In the 'moment' of redemption, one's sins are forgiven, and one is welcomed back to God. In my own case, I had a strong sense of healing: if I didn't necessarily have a strong sense that 'my sins had been forgiven' I had a powerful sense of being returned to God. A breach in God's relationship with me and vice versa had been healed.

There are other pictures of redemption. If modern Christianity has often placed emphasis on individualistic redemption, in which one is supposed to accept Jesus Christ as one's Lord and Saviour, Judaism has traditionally been more focussed on corporate redemption. The book of Exodus shows forth God's promises to the people of Israel, shaped through the prism of Moses. If Moses becomes the focus of God's faithfulness, it is the Hebrews God wishes to set free from bondage in Egypt. Again and again, through the Jewish Bible or Old Testament, God demonstrates his faithfulness to the Covenant by coming to rescue the people of God.

Central to Christian ideas of redemption is the 'saving' work of Jesus Christ. Redemption has monetary or financial overtones. One of its meanings is 'gain or regain possession of something in exchange for payment'. So, a person who has been deprived of their status or rights or position, might regain it by paying a fee or price to the person withholding that status. It is fair to say that the idea that Jesus' death on the Cross 'pays the price for sin' has been and remains controversial. The ancient theologian Origen suggested that Christ pays the price of sin to Satan, thereby buying his people back. This position has generally been rejected, but the claim that something 'transactional' happens on the Cross, through the 'payment' of innocent blood has been remarkably resilient.

Whatever we believe happens on the Cross, the implication is that redemption is the work of God in Christ. In that sense, when I had my conversion experience in the 1990s, all I was doing was recognising a truth. Arguably, I was not redeemed in that moment; rather, I understood that God's redeeming work applied definitively to me too. Indeed, while for much of my life

I'd discounted its value, I came to appreciate that God's redeeming work had exercised a claim over me ever since I'd been baptised as a baby. It was in baptism that my body, my soul, my life had been joined to Christ's redeeming love.

The Greatest Showman is not a religious or Christian film. It certainly isn't interested in foregrounding conversion to Christ or theories of redemption. Yet, it does seem to offer an interesting redemptive trajectory. In previous weeks, we have seen how Barnum finds success and fulfilment and how he is increasingly tempted to betray the communities which have been crucial to that success. His desire to be respectable, leads him to stop thinking about the Circus; his focus on his relationship with Jenny Lind is to the detriment of his family and home life.

In this final study, we explore how Barnum finds a kind of redemption from foolishness. Given his tendency to show embarrassment around the workers in the Circus, it is ironic that it is precisely those Circus performers who manage to save him from himself. Barnum has always sought to be in charge, to 'pay the bills' for his family and friends from his own largesse and cunning, yet it is Circus members who 'buy' him back from his despair. Partly they do that by standing by him at this lowest point and calling him out from his self-pity. Partly it is through Carlyle's sensible and generous approach to his circus life: Carlyle has saved up his part of the Circus' earnings and is prepared to spend it so that the show can begin again.

In short, the Circus members – treated rather shabbily by Barnum – demonstrate an abundant grace, a grace that Barnum hardly deserves. In that sense, they act as surrogates for God. They show forth grace, freely and generously, and invite his response. What is truly fascinating is that Barnum's ultimate response – which involves him stepping away from centre-stage and allowing Carlyle to become the new ringmaster – is a response of grace. It is 'self-emptying'.

That is, in receiving his gift from the Circus, Barnum doesn't need to retake control, but is prepared to let go or empty himself of power. In his *Letter to the Philippians*, St Paul uses this idea of 'kenosis' or 'self-emptying' to speak of God. In chapter 2, Paul suggests that God empties himself of power and authority into the body of Jesus; this self-emptying is a work of letting go. The God of authority and power – the Monarch of the universe, as it were – becomes a mere human being, a peasant in a little out-of-the-way place called Galilee. Yet, this model of grace becomes something that reveals the profound truth of the Way of God: that just as God empties himself, so are we called to love and serve and let go of power-over others for its own sake. Jesus – the very presence of God – does not become a King or Power in the conventional sense. His love is shown in obedience to a criminal's death.

Clearly, Barnum's world is a long way from the theologising of St Paul. However, to our surprise, at the end of *The Greatest Showman*, Barnum has become a greater if not great person. If he is the 'greatest showman' it is no longer simply because he puts on a grand show that makes money from what the critic Bennett might call 'humbug'. Rather, it is because he understands the proper place of the show in living a full and hopeful life. By the close of the film, he has finally gained perspective. He can rejoice in the show and, more importantly, rejoice in his work alongside others. He and the Circus have become friends and equals. It means that he no longer feels the need to be in charge. Equally, he can rejoice in the simple pleasures of family life, enjoying his daughter's love of ballet without needed to feel constricted by societal expectations. He has become the greatest showman because he has stopped being obsessed with the surface. Instead of showing off, he reveals himself to the world. It is a powerful witness and should be a dream and possibility we share in common with him.

OPENING PRAYER

Wondrous God, we thank you for your abundant love
*   which invites us to find the fullness of life in you.*
If we are dust and to dust we shall return,
*   help us to know we are fearfully and wonderfully*
*   made,*
*   crowned with glory and honour.*
Help us to receive faith, hope and love as gift
*   and when we mar your divine image,*
*   may we hear your voice as you call us back home.*
Enable us, through your Spirit, to be people of dreams
*   and visions,*
*   alert to the call of your Kingdom of Grace and*
*   Peace. Amen*

WATCH

Barnum and the ensemble sing 'From Now On' (From: 1:18.50 to 1:25.05)

As he falls to his lowest point, Barnum drinks away his woes in the bar. Then the General and the rest of the ensemble appear to call Barnum to his senses. Lettie tells Barnum, 'Our own mothers were ashamed of us … and now you're giving up on us too … you gave us a real family …', while W.D. says, 'we want our home back.' Together the ensemble sings, 'From Now On', a song which recapitulates all that Barnum, and the others, have and need to be reclaimed.

Think about

Cast your mind back to early in the film. Then, Barnum gives Tom an opportunity to claim some self-respect. To what extent is this scene in the bar a role-reversal of that earlier moment?

How surprising is it that the people of the Circus stand by Barnum after the way he's treated them? What does this reveal about them?

Barnum sings, 'From now on these eyes will not be blinded by the lights'. What has he been unable to see? What has he come to realise? (Have you ever been tempted by what's 'false' rather than what's true?)

The ensemble sings, 'And we will come back home, home again'. What does their idea of 'home' consist in? How does it relate to and differ from yours?

GOING DEEPER

Read
Luke 15:11-32
'The Lost Son'

This is perhaps the most famous parable or story in the entire Bible. It has layers of meaning and a variety of readings. It is first and foremost a story of relationship, tested and reconciled.

The father figure in the parable allows the younger son to leave home, be irresponsible and be a spendthrift with his inheritance. If the 'Circus family' acts as a stand-in for the father of the parable, what are the similarities between Barnum and the Lost Son? Are there differences?

What does this parable teach us about the nature of 'grace' and 'love'? Does the Lost Son deserve the Father's love, after the way the Son behaves? Does Barnum deserve the gracious love of the Circus family?

How does the parable of the Lost Son speak into our own stories? With whom do we most identify in the parable? Why?

WATCH

Barnum and Charity reconciled … (From: 1:25.05 to 1:26.57 mins)

Barnum realises how foolish he has been, and rushes off to his parents-in-law's house to find Charity. Her father says that she isn't there, but Barnum's children tell him, 'She's at the beach'. He finds her where they first shared a 'million dreams'. He acknowledges his faults and confesses that he wanted to be more than he was. Charity says she only ever wanted the man she fell in love with.

Think about

Given all that Barnum has put Charity through, does she accept him back too easily? Explain your response.

Barnum acknowledges that he struggles to accept who he is. Charity says that she never needed him to pretend. How tempting is it to 'big oneself up'? Have you ever done it (on a job application, in conversation etc.)? What were the results?

Why do we struggle to stick to the truth? Is too much truth problematic?

GOING DEEPER

Read
John 21:9-19
'Another beach scene ... Jesus and Peter ...'

This closing section of John's Gospel contains a famous reconciliation scene between Jesus and Peter. On the night of Jesus' betrayal, Peter denied his master three times. In this scene on a beach, Peter finally comes to a definitive place of faithfulness and acceptance. He accepts his call and is reconciled to his Lord.

What does this scene reveal to us about Jesus (the one who has been betrayed and denied by those closest to him)?

How might it feel to be Peter, confronted with his faithlessness and selfishness?

Jesus indicates that Peter's future will involve a difficult path, including death and humiliation. What has changed for Peter that enables him to accept this path?

Both Peter and Barnum have gone astray, only to find their way home to their true calling. How important has their waywardness been for their formation as more complete people? Have you had any similar experiences which have shaped and formed you?

WATCH

A hope rekindled … (From: 1:26.58 to 1.33.07)

The circus pick through the rubble of the circus. Barnum reveals that the bank won't lend any more money. Carlyle says that all he has left is friendship, love and work he adores. Barnum says, 'if only banks would take joy as collateral.' Carlyle reveals he has saved his share of the profits. The deal now is that he and Barnum go fifty-fifty and in partnership they go forward. Instead of occupying a permanent building they become itinerant tent dwellers. In the closing scene, Barnum hands over the ringmaster's role to Carlyle and heads off (on an elephant!) to be with his family. Barnum finally accepts the joy in his life.

Think about

In the reprise of the title song, the ensemble sings, 'The impossible comes true'. To what extent has the impossible come true in the closing scenes?

What do you make of Barnum's decision to retreat from centre-stage and pass the baton on to Carlyle?

Carlyle says that 'all that's left is friendship and love … you brought joy into my life.' Has Carlyle got his priorities right? If so, why? If not, why not?

What place does joy hold in your life? How easy is it experience in the modern world? What gets in the way of receiving the world as gift?

GOING DEEPER

Read
Galatians 5:16-22
'The fruit of the Spirit'

Galatians 5:22 lists the fruit of the Spirit as 'love, joy, peace, patience, kindness, generosity, faithfulness, gentleness and self-control.' By the close of the film, to what extent does Barnum (and the other characters) demonstrate these virtues?

What, in your opinion, is crucial for the fruit of the Spirit to grow in you and the communities of which you are a part?

In 1 Corinthians 13, St Paul suggest that 'faith, hope and love abide, but the greatest of these is love.' To what extent do you agree? Is it the greatest fruit of the Spirit?

St Paul writes, 'If we live by the Spirit, let us be guided by the Spirit. Let us not become conceited, competing against one another, envying one another.' Is this one of the lessons learned by Barnum?

How can we demonstrate the spirit of co-operation rather than the spirit of competition in our church, community and personal lives?

LOOKING AHEAD...
ACTIVITIES TO
CONSIDER THIS
WEEK

What are the things that need to be healed in our lives? Are they relationships with other people (work colleagues, friends, family), or with God? This week, try to focus on the ways you can build up relationships and other people rather than tear them down. If it is appropriate, consider reaching out to someone with whom there has been a damaged or broken-down relationship. In the very least, take some time to pray for healing of broken and damaged relationships.

One practice that can be helpful, especially when it is no longer possible to heal a relationship (perhaps because someone is dead) or to do so would be risky, is write a 'letter never to be sent'. This is where one writes to the person one has hurt or who has hurt us, speaking with utter honesty to them. It is a process which can be profoundly cathartic and revealing. At the end of the process, the letter can symbolically be burned or otherwise destroyed. An alternative practice is to write the letter to God, offering to him the unvarnished truth of one's needs and hopes.

In the Eucharist, or Holy Communion or the Mass, there is a liturgical opportunity to share the Peace. It can be very powerful moment in the liturgy (or a bit of a love-in, or a bit embarrassing, depending on your point of view). If you go to church, try to share the Peace with someone you usual don't, perhaps even someone you struggle with. In your prayers, give thanks to God for the grace you've received from him, and ask that he would continue to convert you towards those with whom you are irritated or struggle with.

CLOSING PRAYER

Gracious God,
   we give thanks for your abundant love
   and the breadth and depth of your forgiveness.
May we who are born in your image
   grow into the likeness of your son Jesus Christ
   and live in joy in your community of love.
You wait for us and call us back home.
Guide and encourage us along your Way of hope,
   and disturb our complacency,
   that we may dare follow you into new life. Amen

POSTSCRIPT

Whether you have followed this study guide as part of a group or as an individual I hope it encourages you to go deeper. Study guides can have that effect. For example, the church where I'm Rector has an afternoon home group that emerged out of a Lent study course half-a-decade ago and now meets month-by-month to study, reflect and pray, often using a film as the focus for study. Darton, Longman and Todd, the publisher of this guide, has many film-based study guides that work throughout the year. While there are many traditional aids to study, there is something very powerful about using visual culture as an aid to reflection on faith. In an age when there is evidence that people are increasingly not interested in long reads, visual culture offers a way to get to the nub of the matter in a concise and engaging way. It's often been said that a picture speaks a thousand words. If that is true, how much more so, does cinema. It offers a mainline into discussion and conversation. Arguably, it also connects us back to earlier expressions of Christianity where the visual was more important than the written. In the Middle Ages, when most people in Europe could not read or write, Christian culture told its stories via vivid pictures and exciting drama. It led to lively and sophisticated lay theologies, something that surely we should be rediscovering at a time when 'discipleship' and 'lay leadership' is the main game in town.

The Greatest Showman is, as I suggested in the introduction, ultimately entertainment. First and foremost, this is how it was meant to be enjoyed and

I hope that this study guide has not taken away from, but enhanced your enjoyment. Nonetheless, as someone who believes that Creation is shot through with grace and sacramental power, I believe it is possible to discern theology in every aspect of the world. I don't mean (I hope) that our calling is to be cheesy and say, when we watch a new film or read a new book, 'Have you noticed that x, y, or z is a little bit like Jesus.' That's a recipe for embarrassment and thin theological reflection.

Rather, most cultural artefacts (even some pretty banal ones) gesture, however dimly, to the great themes of life – love, doubt, redemption and so on. Some do that much better than others and take us much further. The ones that do that are usually called Art. *The Greatest Showman* is never going be counted among the world-changing examples of art. However, like the best musicals, it writes our dreams and hopes large and allows us to locate ourselves in the drama and music it frames. I hope, then, that even if you do not continue to study, pray and reflect using films as a focus, your experience over the past few weeks makes you more alert to God's participation in this remarkable, bruised world we inhabit. May you find God goes with you to the cinema, to the art gallery, to the library, and into all the things you give yourself to.

FROM NOW ON ... LOOKING BACK AND GOING FORWARD FROM HERE

Over the past few weeks, this study guide has examined some large and universal themes. Before we close this book, it is worth reminding ourselves what they were and consider how we might try to go deeper with them in the weeks and months to come:

A MILLION DREAMS ...

As I suggested in Week 1, dreams – waking and sleeping – are part of what it means to be human. In the face of life's challenges and bruises, it can be very challenging to keep dreams alive. One of the key aspects of the Christian life is figuring out what God is calling us towards and into. In Christian prayer, this is often called, 'discernment'. One way of exploring how one can go deeper in discernment is by seeking 'spiritual direction' or 'companionship'. This entails finding someone, trained in prayer, to accompany you in your Christian journey. If you are interested in this, usually Dioceses have lists of trained and approved companions.

Equally, going on retreat to a prayer centre, retreat centre or monastery can be a powerful and transforming experience. If it is your first time on retreat, consider going on a weekend taster. Speak to your minister, diocesan spirituality officer (if you have one) or simply 'google' 'Christian retreat centres' to find out more.

COME ALIVE ...

In the second week, we looked at alternative pictures of family and how those coded as 'other' or as 'outsiders' may be more central to God's agenda than many might suppose. As you go forward, it may be worth thinking how – depending on your personal circumstances – you can be more fully in solidarity with those who are marginalized and excluded. If you have extensive experience of being marginalised, what kind of power can you wield to change your church or local community?

In terms of engaging more fully with transforming church so that it moves from being a place that 'welcomes' those it sees as 'different' to being one which has a celebration of difference at its heart, what can you be involved in? There are numerous projects and organisations like 'Dementia-Friendly Church' or 'Inclusive Church' your community might sign up to. What are the practical steps you might need to address to ensure that, for example, your church is a place that is not run simply for the benefit of its existing members?

REWRITE THE STARS

Campaigning for justice, peace and reconciliation can be tiring and time-consuming. However, as history has repeatedly shown, a small group of determined people can make a difference to the world.

In an age of online petitions and 'hashtag' campaigning, it is easy to mock those who try to change the world via clicking on links. It has even been called 'slacktivism'. Online campaigning is one route to consider, however, if you wish to take the Christian call to justice and peace a little further, consider organising a church-based 'Peace and Justice' group. In some ways, churches – even tiny ones – represent a potentially powerful way of organising and coordinating campaigning. Alternatively, large organisations like Amnesty International offer a ready means to coordinate campaigning.

For those who feel certain forms of campaigning are too politicized, there are other options. Perhaps it is time to revisit your church's commitment to Fairtrade; perhaps you could consider volunteering with your local foodbank or acting as your church's coordinator for your Harvest collection and so on. Crucially, get involved!

NEVER ENOUGH

If there is a pressing crisis in our world it centres around 'climate change' and the future of this beautiful, fragile planet. Our society – consumerist and capitalist – tells us that we are what we can buy or afford; it says that we can never have enough. There are few greater challenges than living simply in our society.

Perhaps it is time for each of us to find ways to simplify our lives. It is certainly something that many of Christianity's greatest figures, including St Francis, would encourage in us. There are many possible strategies to consider. Some have sought to reduce the amount of single-use plastic in their lives. Equally, perhaps it is time for all of us to become 'reductitarians', where we normalise not eating meat so often.

Churches represent, as previously suggested, communities where joint action can have real effects. It will send a powerful signal to wider communities if our churches commit to stop using plastic where practicable. What are the other ways our churches can reduce their carbon imprint? What are, for example, the health impacts of more of us walking, cycling or car-sharing when we go to church?

FROM NOW ON

A friend recently told me that she increasingly struggles to feel joy and delight. The world has become so challenging and problematic and the demands on our time and resources so great that it is possible to feel endlessly guilty. The pressure to be an activist all the time can strip us of pleasure, fun and delight.

So, please, do not exhaust yourself with pious and relentless enthusiasm! As we see at the end of *The Greatest Showman*, it is also important to be open to receive joy and delight. This world is God's world and it is therefore gift. All that we have, as Barnum discovers, is gift, for which we should be thankful. Yes, we should not be smug and complacent about it (and we should dare to share what we have with others), but if we are serious and pious all the time, then we are not being faithful to God.

So, above all, do not be afraid to enjoy God's creation. Whatever else we do, in the season of Easter and beyond, we are called to rejoice in the gift of God's love and grace. It is his dream for us and it is our joy to respond with delight.